THE STORY OF THE DALLAS MAVERICKS

THE NBA: A HISTORY OF HOOPS

THE STORY OF THE
DALLAS MAVERICKS

NATE FRISCH

CREATIVE EDUCATION

Published by Creative Education
P.O. Box 227, Mankato, Minnesota 56002
Creative Education is an imprint of The Creative Company
www.thecreativecompany.us

Design and production by Blue Design
Art direction by Rita Marshall
Printed in the United States of America

Photographs by Corbis (Steve Lipofsky, John F. Rhodes/
Dallas Morning News), Getty Images (Bill Baptist/
NBAE, Walter Bibikow, John Biever/Sports Illustrated,
Kevork Djansezian, Stephen Dunn, Jesse D. Garrabrant/
NBAE, Otto Greule Jr./Allsport, Glenn James/NBAE,
Fernando Medina/NBAE, Layne Murdoch/NBAE, Doug
Pensinger, Mike Powell, Dick Raphael/NBAE), Newscom
(Mark Halmas/Icon SMI 483, Ron Jenkins/MCT, Jose Luis
Villegas/ZUMA Press, Brandon Wade/MCT)

Library of Congress Cataloging-in-Publication Data
Frisch, Nate.
The story of the Dallas Mavericks / Nate Frisch.
p. cm. — (The NBA: a history of hoops)
Includes index.
Summary: An informative narration of the Dallas
Mavericks professional basketball team's history from its
1980 founding to today, spotlighting memorable players
and reliving dramatic events.
ISBN 978-1-60818-427-9
1. Dallas Mavericks (Basketball team)—History—Juvenile
literature. I. Title.

GV885.52.D34F755 2014
796.323'64097642812—dc23   2013037446

CCSS: RI.5.1, 2, 3, 8; RH.6-8.4, 5, 7

First Edition
9 8 7 6 5 4 3 2 1

Cover: Guard Monta Ellis
Pages 2 & 5: Forward Shawn Marion
Page 6: Guard Tariq Abdul-Wahad

TABLE OF CONTENTS

COURTSIDE STORIES

INTRODUCING...

BREAKING NEW GROUND

THE CITY OF DALLAS, TEXAS, HAS A HISTORY OF SUCCESSFUL PRO SPORTS TEAMS.

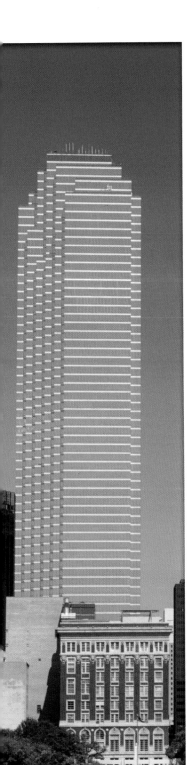

When the United States was expanding westward in the early 1800s, settlers often had little means of acquiring necessary supplies. Recognizing this, risk-taking entrepreneurs would sometimes strike out ahead of the crowds and develop outposts where the settlers could buy supplies, recuperate from hard travel, and experience some measure of civilization in the Old West. John Neely Bryan was one such entrepreneur, and he developed the town of Dallas, Texas, in 1839. As years passed, Dallas evolved from a small-scale trading, farming, and ranching settlement into a major distribution center for the oil and cotton industries. Today, the Dallas–Fort Worth–Arlington area comprises the fourth-largest metropolitan area in the U.S. and is the base camp for companies such as

SINCE THEIR VERY FIRST TIPOFF, THE "MAVS" HAVE ENJOYED A LOYAL FAN BASE IN TEXAS.

ExxonMobil, Texas Instruments, and Frito-Lay.

As the population of the Dallas area steadily increased, so did the desire for various forms of sports and recreation. In 1960, the National Football League's Dallas Cowboys were created. Twelve years later, the Texas Rangers of Major League Baseball moved into Arlington. Businessman Donald J. Carter believed the area's avid fan base could support another pro sports club and pushed to get a National Basketball Association (NBA) franchise created in Dallas. The 1980 expansion club was named the Mavericks—a term that can describe either independent-thinking people or rogue cattle, and Dallas's history involved plenty of both.

The Mavericks hoped to combine innovative thinking with bullish power as they headed into their first season. Their head coach was Dick Motta, who had led the Washington Bullets to the NBA championship three seasons earlier.

SAM PERKINS

TWO FOR THE PRICE OF ONE

Each year, every team in the NBA puts a lot of thought and research into its first-round pick in the NBA Draft. The higher the pick, the more important it is. In 1980, the Dallas Mavericks were granted the 11th overall draft selection, which in theory meant they could get the 11th-best player available from the college ranks and make him the cornerstone of their new franchise. The Mavs chose high-scoring forward Kiki Vandeweghe from UCLA. Vandeweghe, however, had no intention of signing with a fledgling franchise and immediately demanded to be traded. It was a tough blow to take, but the Mavericks set out to make the best of the situation. In December 1980, they traded the rights to Vandeweghe (plus their 1986 first-round draft choice) to the Nuggets for two future first-round draft picks. With those picks, the Mavs selected guard Rolando Blackman in 1981 and center Sam Perkins in 1984. Perkins became a solid performer at forward for six years in Dallas, and as of 2014, Blackman was the second-most prolific scorer in Mavericks history.

INTRODUCING...

MARK AGUIRRE

POSITION FORWARD / GUARD
HEIGHT 6-FOOT-6
MAVERICKS SEASONS
1981–89

Sometimes it's helpful for a basketball team to have a player with a nasty side. Before the Mavericks made Mark Aguirre from DePaul University the number-one overall pick in the 1981 NBA Draft, they'd seen his skills on the court, and they'd heard about his sometimes surly attitude. Aguirre was never a player who went out of his way to be the most-liked player in the NBA, but what he did do was score. At 6-foot-6 and 235 pounds, he was considerably stockier than the league's prototypical player. Over the course of his career, he averaged 20 points per game, and as of 2014, he held the Mavericks' single-season scoring record with 2,330 points (in 1983–84). On several occasions, the prickly star butted heads with coach Dick Motta, but in the end, Aguirre's scoring ability kept the Mavericks and their fans happy. "He was a passer, he was a power player inside, and he played against bigger people," said Dallas coach John MacLeod. "And then he had the ability to drive the ball to the basket. He was a complete player."

"DEREK IS ALWAYS READY TO PLAY AT THE END OF A BASKETBALL GAME. HE'S WILLING TO BE A HERO. HE'S WILLING TO BE A GOAT—HE DOESN'T CARE. YOU'VE GOT TO GET THE BASKETBALL TO GUYS LIKE THAT."

— ROLANDO BLACKMAN ON TEAMMATE DEREK HARPER

However, Motta initially struggled to build a competitive roster in Dallas. The team selected proven veterans in guard Austin Carr and forward Richard Washington in the expansion draft, but neither would spend more than 11 games in a Mavericks uniform.

Dallas had similar problems when it tried to add collegiate talent. After Kiki Vandeweghe was chosen in the 1980 NBA Draft, the forward refused to join the "Mavs" and was traded away for future draft selections. The product that ultimately hit the court in 1980–81 was underwhelming. The only long-term talent to come out of an ugly 15–67 inaugural campaign was point guard Brad Davis, who averaged 11.2 points and 6.9 assists that season.

Dallas then selected three talented rookies in the 1981 NBA Draft: guard Rolando Blackman, swingman Mark Aguirre, and forward Jay Vincent. Blackman proved to be a fierce defender and a great outside shooter, while Aguirre and Vincent gave the team plenty of inside muscle. With the addition of these youngsters, the Mavericks showed quick and dramatic improvement, leaping to 28–54 in 1981–82 and 38–44 the following season. Things were beginning to look up in "Big D."

In 1983, the Mavericks continued to enjoy tremendous success in the NBA Draft, adding guard Derek Harper. Harper had incredibly quick hands, which made him one of the league's best defenders. After spending his first few NBA seasons backing up Davis, he would become a permanent part of Dallas's starting lineup. "Derek is always ready to play at the end of a basketball game," said Blackman. "He's willing to be a hero. He's willing to be a goat—he doesn't care. You've got to get the basketball to guys like that."

DICK MOTTA

COACH
MAVERICKS SEASONS
1980–87,
1994–96

Dick Motta claimed to have never even seen an NBA game in person before signing his first NBA coaching contract in 1968. Regardless, he was the 1971 NBA Coach of the Year with the Chicago Bulls and won a championship in 1978 with the Washington Bullets. So when the fledgling Dallas Mavericks looked for their very first head coach, they tabbed him for the job. Although his players towered over him, the fiery Motta was a coach who demanded respect. In his interactions with the media, however, a more playful side of his personality often came out. "About three days into the training camp," he said of his first days with the expansion Mavericks franchise, "I was hoping that I could take some type of time tablet and play Rip Van Winkle, and have someone wake me up in three or four years!" By his fourth season as the Mavericks' coach, Motta had transformed Dallas into a playoff contender. Among the NBA's 10 winningest coaches of all time (as of 2014), Motta led the Mavs to the playoffs 4 times and oversaw the drafting of some of Dallas's most beloved stars.

MAVS SHOW
THEIR HORNS

ROLANDO BLACKMAN'S ABILITY TO FOLLOW THROUGH MADE HIM AN ALL-TIME SCORING LEADER.

The Mavericks' improved talent level led to a rise in the Western Conference's Midwest Division standings. Dallas ended the 1983–84 season with the first winning record (43–39) in franchise history. That finish was good enough for second place in the division and earned the Mavericks their first playoff berth. Dallas beat the Seattle SuperSonics three games to two (winning Game 5 in overtime) in round one of postseason play. The Mavs' second-round opponent, however, was the scorching-hot Los Angeles Lakers, who defeated Dallas on their way to the NBA Finals.

The next year, the Mavericks drafted long-armed forward/center Sam Perkins, who soon proved to be a force with his solid rebounding effort and knack for swatting away opposing shots. The team made the playoffs again with a 44–38 record but lost to the Portland Trail Blazers in the first round.

Early in the 1985–86 season, the Mavs traded for center James Donaldson. At a massive 7-foot-2, Donaldson gave Dallas intimidating size and strength in the low post. With his addition, the Mavs again went 44–38, and then whipped the Utah Jazz in the first round of the playoffs before falling to the mighty Lakers in round two.

By 1986, Mavericks fans had grown accustomed to watching their team win during the regular season but get bounced from the playoffs. When the Mavs drafted towering forward Roy Tarpley, though, hopes rose. And when the Mavs' loaded lineup went 55–27 in 1986–87 and won the Midwest Division, an NBA championship seemed within reach. The excitement in Dallas came to an early and bitter halt, though, as the Mavs lost to the SuperSonics, three games to one, in a first-round playoff upset.

After that painful defeat, Motta stepped down as head coach and was replaced by John MacLeod, who soon made Tarpley the team's sixth man. By coming off the bench late in the game, Tarpley often dominated his tired opponents. "With Roy on the floor, we talk NBA championship," said Blackman. "He brings us that little piece of magic ... you see in a player who is superior to everyone he plays against."

In the 1988 playoffs, Tarpley and the Mavs earned victories over the Houston Rockets and Denver Nuggets. The only team standing between them and the NBA Finals was their old nemesis, the Lakers. In a titanic battle, the two teams split the first six games of the Western Conference finals, but the more experienced Lakers won Game 7 by a 117–102 score. Los Angeles went on to win the NBA championship,

while the Mavs again went home empty-handed.

Still, Dallas fans were as enthusiastic as ever heading into the 1988–89 season. Their team had made the playoffs five straight years, getting achingly close to the NBA Finals every time. But then everything fell apart. First, Tarpley was suspended for drug abuse. Then Aguirre demanded to be traded and was dealt to the Detroit Pistons for a player—forward Adrian Dantley—who at first refused to play for Dallas. To top it all off, Donaldson suffered a serious knee injury.

In just a few weeks, the team chemistry that Dallas had worked so long to build was almost completely destroyed. Even though Dantley eventually suited up for Dallas and Tarpley returned from his suspension, the damage was done. The Mavericks missed the 1989 playoffs, made a brief comeback the next season with a 47–35 record, and then suffered a first-round playoff exit. Little did Dallas fans know that their team was about to fall into a long, agonizing slump and that the Mavericks wouldn't make the playoffs again for more than a decade.

INTRODUCING...

ROLANDO BLACKMAN

POSITION GUARD
HEIGHT 6-FOOT-6
MAVERICKS SEASONS
1981–92

When the Mavericks selected Rolando Blackman ninth overall in the 1981 NBA Draft, Dallas was a young team that badly needed a hero. It found one in the slick-shooting guard from Kansas State University. High-strung and always intense, Blackman was never lacking in confidence. As an unproven rookie, he boldly predicted that he'd be a star and that he couldn't be guarded. He became a great scorer, but his intensity made him a tenacious defensive player as well. Blackman helped to form the foundation of a Mavericks team that was consistently a force to be reckoned with in the mid-1980s. From 1984 to 1990, the Mavericks missed the playoffs only once, while Blackman earned All-Star status four times. Blackman retired as the Mavericks' all-time leading scorer after 11 seasons with the team and 2 more with the New York Knicks. Lakers Hall-of-Famer Magic Johnson recalled playing against Blackman, calling him "one of the greatest shooters of all time and one of the most difficult players to guard." It turned out that Blackman's prediction had been as accurate as his shot.

AN EXPLOSIVE OVERTIME

Sometimes NBA fans get more than they pay for. When the Mavericks faced their intrastate rivals, the Houston Rockets, on April 11, 1995, Dallas was 34–41 and considered an underdog to the 44-32 Rockets. On this night, however, the two teams were evenly matched. The Mavericks pulled away and appeared headed for a comfortable victory before the Rockets rallied to score 18 points in the final 70 seconds of regulation to tie the game at 119–119. In the first overtime, it was the Mavericks' turn to erupt. They scored 11 points in the last 55 seconds, including a trio of 3-point shots from guard Jason Kidd, to send the game into double overtime. The Mavericks rode that wave of momentum to defeat the Rockets by a final score of 156–147. The two teams combined for 46 points in the first overtime period, which remained an NBA record as of 2014. "I've never played in a game like this," said a tired Kidd. "I hope it will be the last."

JASON KIDD

MAVS IN THE MUCK

Despite the best efforts of such players as rugged rebounder Terry Davis, Dallas became a basketball disaster in the early '90s, plunging from a 28–54 record in 1990–91 to an embarrassing 11-71 in 1992-93. The Mavs parted ways with aging, oft-injured veterans in hopes of building for the future. Unfortunately, though, the team's youth and lack of leadership was evident in its play, and the club simply couldn't compete in a league where experience and teamwork were every bit as important as athleticism. Only late-season victories each year through 1994 kept the Mavericks from setting a new NBA record for the fewest wins in a season.

The only silver lining to the Mavs' horrible seasons of the early '90s was that, by finishing at the bottom of the standings, the team consistently "earned" high picks in

COURTSIDE STORIES

A DRAFT-DAY STEAL

Where does a team look when it wants to make a steal of a trade? Why not to the team that traded legendary center Kareem Abdul-Jabbar away in 1975? Or the team that drafted highflying forward Julius "Dr. J" Erving, only to watch him slip through its fingers in 1972? The Milwaukee Bucks were on the unfortunate end of both of those deals, and in 1998, they were willing to swap again. Dallas orchestrated a three-team trade that gave Milwaukee the rights to the sixth pick in that year's NBA Draft, which the Mavs had used to grab beefy University of Michigan forward Robert "Tractor" Traylor. The Mavericks ended up with the rights to forwards Dirk Nowitzki and Pat Garrity. Dallas immediately turned around and traded Garrity to the Phoenix Suns for point guard Steve Nash. Garrity became a solid bench player for a decade, and Traylor assembled a mediocre seven-year NBA career. Nash, meanwhile, tallied a whopping 2,919 career assists in a Dallas uniform, and Nowitzki went on to win the 2007 NBA MVP award, making the blockbuster deal a major steal for the Mavericks.

the annual NBA Draft. Dallas used these picks to stockpile some of the nation's best college players. From 1992 to 1994, the Mavs drafted three outstanding young players: guard Jim Jackson, forward Jamal Mashburn, and point guard Jason Kidd.

In 1994–95, the Mavs at last showed signs of life by assembling a respectable 36–46 mark. Part of the credit went to such players as big forward Popeye Jones. The driving force behind this improvement, however, was the team's "Three J's"—Jim, Jamal, and Jason. Jackson and Mashburn combined to score almost 50 points a game, while Kidd dished out 7.7 assists per game and was named NBA Co-Rookie of the Year (along with Pistons forward Grant Hill).

At 6-foot-4 and 205 pounds, Kidd could do it all: run the fast break, score, rebound, and

ROY TARPLEY'S SOLID PLAY WAS UNDERMINED BY INJURY AND SUSPENSION.

A GLOBAL GAME

Thanks in part to the enormous following of the U.S. Olympic "Dream Teams" during the 1992 and 1996 Summer Olympics, basketball's global popularity was soaring by the end of the 1990s. Fourteen international players were chosen in the 2000 NBA Draft, and 45 were taken the next year. Perhaps no team embraced the multinational blending of the NBA like the Dallas Mavericks. When the Mavs took the court for the 2001–02 season, they featured one of the most nationally diverse rosters in league history. Their slick-passing point guard, Steve Nash, hailed from Canada (though he was actually born in South Africa). The team's star forward, Dirk Nowitzki, was from Germany and manned the frontcourt with Chinese center Wang Zhizhi. Mexican forward Eduardo Najera and French guard Tariq Abdul-Wahad, meanwhile, rounded out what was a very talented team. "Having players that are national heroes adds quite a bit to the team," Mavericks owner Mark Cuban said of his squad. "Having a whole country counting on you to represent them and win is a whole lot more pressure than an NBA playoff game."

"HE'S GOING TO BE OUR POINT GUARD. HE'LL BE TERRIFIC IN OUR SYSTEM."

— DON NELSON ON ACQUIRING STEVE NASH

shut down opposing guards on the defensive end of the court. Even Chicago Bulls star guard Michael Jordan called Kidd "the future" of the NBA. In 1995–96, Kidd backed up the hype by averaging 16.6 points and 9.7 assists—many of them in alley-oop, behind-the-back, or "no-look" fashion—per game.

Sadly, this great collection of talent would largely go to waste. Mashburn suffered a serious knee injury in 1995, and personality clashes among players began to tear the team apart. In 1996, Dallas hired a new coach, Jim Cleamons, and installed a new half-court offense. Kidd, who preferred a faster-paced offense that allowed him to create plays in the open court, did not adapt well to the change. In a rapid series of stunning moves, the Mavericks traded away Kidd, Mashburn, and Jackson. When the dust settled, several new faces were visible: most notably 7-foot-6 center Shawn Bradley and high-scoring swingman Michael Finley.

In an entertaining yet frustrating 1997–98 season, the Mavericks pulled off a number of upsets under new coach Don Nelson but could muster only 20 wins en route to losing 62 games. During the off-season, Nelson and the Mavs began to pursue players around whom they could construct a winning lineup. In a trade with the Phoenix Suns, Dallas found one such player, securing a proven on-court leader by acquiring guard Steve Nash. "He's going to be our point guard," promised Nelson. "He'll be terrific in our system."

DEREK HARPER

POSITION GUARD
HEIGHT 6-FOOT-4
MAVERICKS SEASONS
1983–94

Some players help their team without having superstar statistics. They're sometimes called the "glue guys," because they're the players who hold a team together. For 10 seasons, Derek Harper was a glue guy for the Dallas Mavericks. On a team that featured the volatile Mark Aguirre and the overly energetic Rolando Blackman, Harper provided steady scoring and steely defense. Whenever the Mavs would face a superstar guard, shutting him down would be Harper's assignment. In 1986, he became the first Dallas player ever named to the NBA's All-Defensive team. In typical glue-guy fashion, if something broke, Harper found a way to fix it. Late in Game 4 of the second round of the 1984 playoffs, he made an embarrassing mistake by dribbling out the clock, thinking that the Mavericks were leading the Lakers when, in fact, the game was tied. The Lakers went on to win. Two years later, in another round-two matchup against the Lakers, Harper made up for it by draining two three-pointers in the final minute of Game 3 to win the game and keep the Mavericks alive in the series.

CUBAN RAISES THE BAR

BIG MAN DIRK NOWITZKI HAD THE ABILITY TO SCORE FROM EVERY ANGLE.

The 1998–99 season didn't actually begin until February 5, 1999, as NBA owners and players argued over salary issues. Although the Mavericks finished that abbreviated season with a subpar 19–31 record, they gave their fans a good showing, going 15–10 at home.

Finley stepped up his game in 1999–2000, averaging 22.6 points, 5.3 assists, and 6.3 rebounds per game. Second-year forward Dirk Nowitzki, meanwhile, was proving to be a dangerous three-point bomber as well as a formidable low-post scorer. Dallas finished with another losing record, 40–42, but its 30–18 mark over the second half of the season brought real hope to the Mavericks faithful for the first time since the Three J's era.

Playing under new team owner Mark Cuban, the Mavs finally broke their playoff drought in 2000-01. After trading

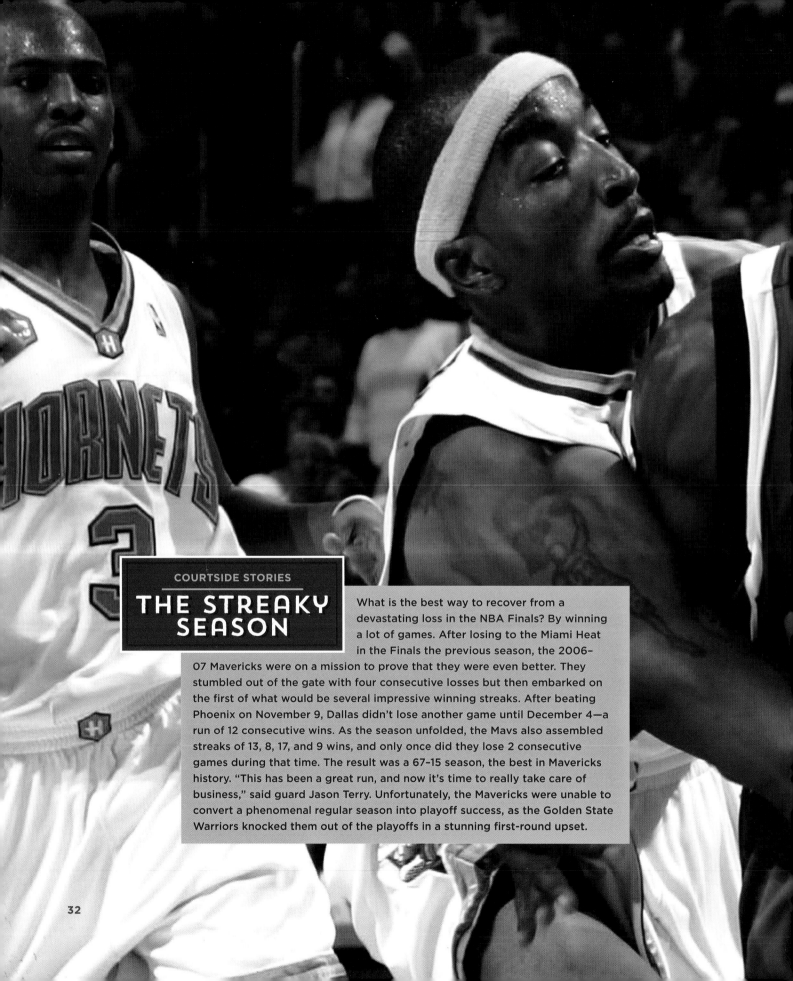

THE STREAKY SEASON

What is the best way to recover from a devastating loss in the NBA Finals? By winning a lot of games. After losing to the Miami Heat in the Finals the previous season, the 2006–07 Mavericks were on a mission to prove that they were even better. They stumbled out of the gate with four consecutive losses but then embarked on the first of what would be several impressive winning streaks. After beating Phoenix on November 9, Dallas didn't lose another game until December 4—a run of 12 consecutive wins. As the season unfolded, the Mavs also assembled streaks of 13, 8, 17, and 9 wins, and only once did they lose 2 consecutive games during that time. The result was a 67–15 season, the best in Mavericks history. "This has been a great run, and now it's time to really take care of business," said guard Jason Terry. Unfortunately, the Mavericks were unable to convert a phenomenal regular season into playoff success, as the Golden State Warriors knocked them out of the playoffs in a stunning first-round upset.

JASON TERRY

33

SHAWN BRADLEY'S FAR-REACHING 7-FOOT-6 WINGSPAN FRUSTRATED HIS SMALLER OPPONENTS.

for veteran forward Juwon Howard, Dallas cruised to a 53–29 mark. In the postseason, the starting five of Nash, Finley, Nowitzki, Howard, and Bradley led the Mavericks past the Utah Jazz in the first round but were unable to conquer the San Antonio Spurs in round two. The Mavericks, though, were about to run.

The Mavs tipped off 2001–02 in a new home, having left Reunion Arena for the state-of-the-art American Airlines Center, and Dallas fans had reason to believe their Mavericks might decorate their new digs with a championship banner. In midseason, the Mavs sent Howard and two other players to the Nuggets for forward Raef LaFrentz and guards Nick Van Exel and Avery Johnson. With these players supporting the three-pronged attack of Nash, Nowitzki, and Finley, the Mavericks surged to 57 wins. They swept the Minnesota Timberwolves in the first round but fell short of the NBA Finals again as the Sacramento Kings then defeated them four games to one.

DIRK NOWITZKI

POSITION FORWARD
HEIGHT 7 FEET
MAVERICKS SEASONS
1998–PRESENT

Some players excel through astounding grace and athleticism, and others simply get things done. Often compared to Boston Celtics Hall-of-Famer Larry Bird, Dirk Nowitzki was rarely, if ever, the fastest, highest-jumping, or most athletic player on the court. He was, however, very agile for a seven-footer and deadly accurate from three-point range, which could wreak havoc on opposing defenses. Hailing from Germany, Nowitzki played smart and could pass, shoot, or get in the paint to grab rebounds and earn second-chance shots. His unselfish, "pass-first" mentality was admirable, but his coaches urged him early on to be more aggressive and accept his role as a scoring leader. Nowitzki learned quickly. In 2007, he was the first European-born player ever to be named NBA MVP, and on March 8, 2008, he surpassed former Mavs great Rolando Blackman as Dallas's all-time leading scorer with his 16,644th point. Even one of the NBA's most legendary centers, Shaquille O'Neal, admired the versatility of Nowitzki's game, saying, "When they talk about great big men, it'll be based on if guys can play like Dirk or not. He's the future."

"IT WAS A MATTER OF THEM TURNING THEIR GEAR UP A LEVEL, AND WE COULDN'T GET ANY HIGHER. THAT WAS THE END OF IT."

— COACH DON NELSON ON THE 2003 PLAYOFFS AGAINST THE SPURS

The Mavs continued their upward climb in 2002-03, cruising to a 60-22 record—tied for the best in the NBA with the Spurs. After defeating the Trail Blazers in the first round of the playoffs, the Mavericks knocked out the Kings in seven games to advance to the Western Conference finals for the first time since 1988. Unfortunately, the Spurs proved to be too much for the Mavericks, and Dallas fell four games to two. "It was a matter of them turning their gear up a level, and we couldn't get any higher," explained Coach Nelson. "That was the end of it."

nce forwards Antoine Walker and Antawn Jamison arrived, opposing defenses could no longer worry about just three Mavs stars: Nash, Nowitzki, Finley, Jamison, and Walker each scored 14 or more points per game in 2003-04. For the 4th season in a row, Dallas won more than 50 games, but the Mavs continued to stumble in the postseason as the Kings sent them home in the first round.

True to form, the Mavericks prepared for the next season by packing off Jamison and Walker, and Nash returned to Phoenix as a free agent. Guard Jason Terry and forward Jerry Stackhouse were brought in via trades, and Dallas obtained fast point guard Devin Harris in the NBA Draft. With improved play from second-year forward Josh Howard, the Mavericks put together a 58-24 record to earn a fifth consecutive playoff appearance. Unfortunately, after defeating the Rockets in seven games in the first round, the Mavericks were bested by Nash and the Suns in the second round.

DEVIN HARRIS CONFIDENTLY CHARGED THE BASKET, EVEN WHEN HE WAS UP AGAINST BIGGER VETERANS.

SIXTH MAN JERRY STACKHOUSE'S FEISTY OFFENSE ADDED DEPTH FROM THE BENCH.

STAMPEDING TO GLORY

THE VERSATILE JOSH HOWARD PROPELLED THE MAVS TO THEIR FIRST NBA FINALS.

As much as fans appreciated the fact that Dallas was winning 50-plus games each season, the playoff lapses in early rounds were hard to accept. Going into 2005–06, Avery Johnson would begin his first full season as head coach. Johnson asked Terry to focus more on scoring and assigned primary ball-handling duties to Harris. Howard continued to improve, and Nowitzki cemented his status as one of the league's top players, averaging 26.6 points and 9.0 rebounds per game. Dallas rolled to a 60–22 record and bested the Memphis Grizzlies, the defending champion Spurs, and the Suns in the playoffs to reach the NBA Finals at last.

Mavericks fans could almost taste NBA glory when their team overwhelmed the Miami Heat in the first two games of the 2006 Finals. But the Heat, who were led by

electrifying young guard Dwyane Wade and massive center Shaquille O'Neal, then left Dallas hungry by storming back to win the next four games. The collapse was painful, but for the young coach and his players, the future still held great promise. "We aimed high this year, and I told my players that a lot of teams have to go through this," Johnson said. "This will really hurt this summer, but I'm ready to try it again."

The next season, Dallas dominated on its way to a 67–15 record. Howard had risen to All-Star status, and Nowitzki earned the league Most Valuable Player (MVP) trophy, but the Mavericks had their sights set on another trophy. In the first round of the 2007 playoffs, Dallas was matched up against the Golden State Warriors, the lowest-seeded team in the Western

Conference and a perennial pushover for more than a decade. But the Warriors, led by coach Don Nelson, shocked Dallas and the NBA, taking the Mavericks down four games to two. "It's a disappointment. You can't even describe it," said Nowitzki. "You play your heart out for 6, 7 months, you win 67 games, and it really means nothing at this point. This is tough to swallow."

In 2007–08, as Harris was having his best season yet, Dallas traded the young guard to the New Jersey Nets in a blockbuster deal that brought point guard Jason Kidd back to the Mavericks. Kidd wasn't as quick as Harris, but the savvy veteran was an unshakable floor general. The team made the playoffs with a 51–31 record but was once again knocked out in the first round. The Mavericks seemed to

MARK CUBAN

TEAM OWNER
MAVERICKS SEASONS
2000–PRESENT

It's every sports fan's dream. Not only do you get to cheer for your favorite team, but you have the financial means to buy it and do your best to make it a winner. After making himself a billionaire by creating and selling Internet companies, Mark Cuban purchased the Dallas Mavericks franchise in 2000 and quickly became one of the most talked-about owners in all of sports. Never an owner who was content to sit in a luxury box and complain quietly about the lack of talent on his team, Cuban boldly went after expensive talent on the free-agent market and could regularly be seen cheering himself hoarse from his courtside seat. Cuban was never shy about speaking his mind, and he was fined more than $1 million by the NBA for public gripes about referees and other league criticisms. Yet no matter what people thought of Cuban's volatile nature, they couldn't deny his passion or success. The Mavericks made the playoffs each of the first 12 full years under his ownership and won their first NBA title in 2011. "Mark came along at our darkest hour and pulled this franchise up," said Dallas coach Don Nelson.

IN HIS SHORT TIME WITH THE MAVERICKS, FORWARD TIM THOMAS PROVED HIS SOFT TOUCH.

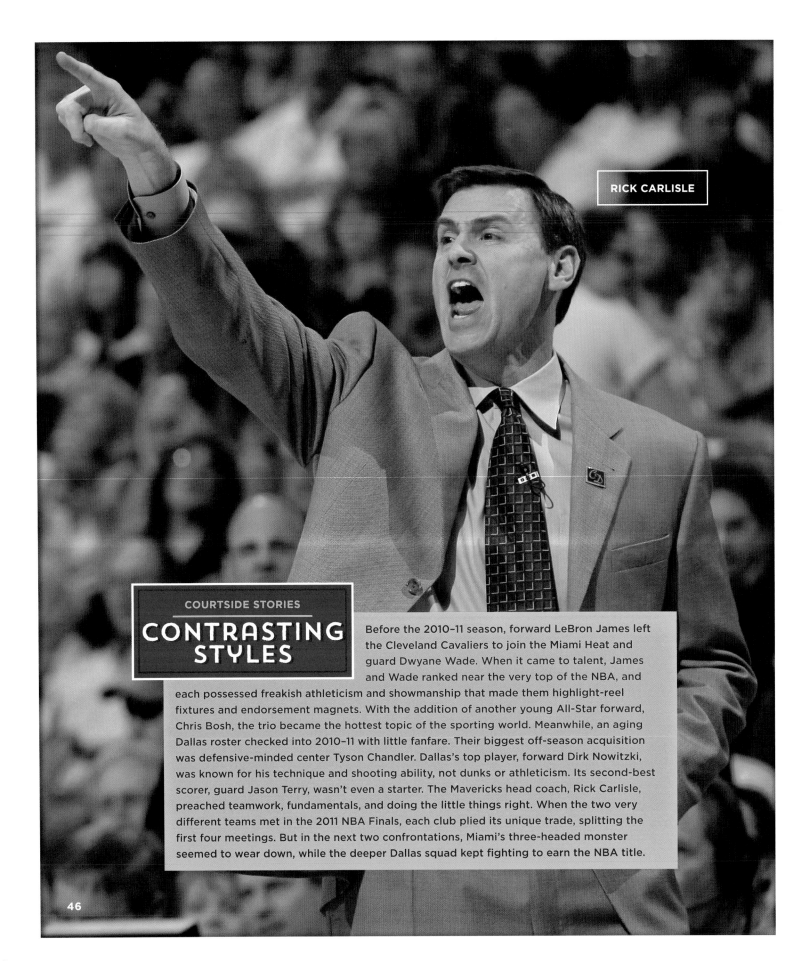

RICK CARLISLE

CONTRASTING STYLES

Before the 2010–11 season, forward LeBron James left the Cleveland Cavaliers to join the Miami Heat and guard Dwyane Wade. When it came to talent, James and Wade ranked near the very top of the NBA, and each possessed freakish athleticism and showmanship that made them highlight-reel fixtures and endorsement magnets. With the addition of another young All-Star forward, Chris Bosh, the trio became the hottest topic of the sporting world. Meanwhile, an aging Dallas roster checked into 2010–11 with little fanfare. Their biggest off-season acquisition was defensive-minded center Tyson Chandler. Dallas's top player, forward Dirk Nowitzki, was known for his technique and shooting ability, not dunks or athleticism. Its second-best scorer, guard Jason Terry, wasn't even a starter. The Mavericks head coach, Rick Carlisle, preached teamwork, fundamentals, and doing the little things right. When the two very different teams met in the 2011 NBA Finals, each club plied its unique trade, splitting the first four meetings. But in the next two confrontations, Miami's three-headed monster seemed to wear down, while the deeper Dallas squad kept fighting to earn the NBA title.

be spinning their wheels, and after the playoff failure, Coach Johnson was replaced by veteran coach Rick Carlisle. Over the next two seasons, Dallas added steady veteran forward Shawn Marion and traded away Howard. The Mavs posted at least 50 victories for the 9th and 10th seasons in a row, but they suffered playoff defeats each time.

The 2010–11 season would soon set things right. It began with a trade that brought 7-foot-1 Tyson Chandler to Dallas. The veteran center was not a great offensive threat, but he excelled at challenging shots and working the boards. The big man was named to the NBA All-Defensive team, and a balanced team effort led Dallas to a 57–25 record.

n the postseason, Dallas defeated first the Trail Blazers, then the Lakers, and then the Oklahoma City Thunder to confront the Heat again in the Finals. The Heat had been the most publicized team in the league that season after All-Star forwards LeBron James and Chris Bosh had joined the club to form a dynamic trio with Dallas nemesis Dwyane Wade. Dallas and Miami split the first four games of the series. Then Dallas won the next meeting by nine. In Game 6, Nowitzki grabbed 11 boards and Terry poured in 27 points as the Mavericks earned a 105–95 victory. The club that had been knocking on the door for 11 straight seasons finally barged into NBA lore with its first championship. "This is a true team," Carlisle said after claiming the NBA title. "This is an old bunch. We don't run fast or jump high. [But] these guys had each other's backs. We played the right way…. This is a phenomenal thing for the city of Dallas."

Naturally, expectations were high going into

2011–12, but labor disputes between players and owners delayed the season tipoff by about two months. To make up for lost time, the NBA tried to pack as many games as possible into the condensed schedule. The rigorous itinerary seemed to take its toll on older clubs, and after Dallas went 36–30 in the regular season, it was immediately swept out of the playoffs by the much younger Thunder.

Going into the 2012–13 campaign, Nowitzki was shelved following knee surgery, and Kidd, Terry, and Chandler had all left town. Brought in were speedy young guards O. J. Mayo and Darren Collison. The duo upped the tempo but couldn't stem Dallas's decline, and the Mavs missed the playoffs for the first time in 13 years. But with the daring Cuban calling the shots, Dallas figured to be back among the contenders very soon. "Our goal is to win championships, so it's disappointing to not win," said Cuban. "But we will come back and get better next year."

Hoping to do just that, Dallas signed guard Monta "Mississippi Bullet" Ellis before the start of the 2013–14 season. Although Collison left for Los Angeles, Nowitzki was back to form and appeared in his 12th All-Star Game. As he continued to move up the list of all-time leading NBA scorers, fans eagerly awaited each game in 2014.

Dallas has never been the town for the timid. Gutsy leader Derek Harper, clutch shooter Dirk Nowitzki, and bold owner Mark Cuban have left their brands on the city by being true mavericks. Today's Mavericks are not content with past achievements, though. The page may be turning on one title-winning bunch of Dallas greats, but Mavs fans expect big things in the next chapter as well.

INDEX